www.raintreepublishers.co.uk
Visit our website to find out more information about **Raintree** books.
To order:
☎ Phone 44 (0)1865 888113
🖹 Send a fax to 44 (0)1865 314091
💻 Visit the Raintree bookshop at **www.raintreepublishers.co.uk** to browse
our catalogue and order online.

First published in Great Britain by Raintree, Halley Court, Jordan Hill, Oxford OX2 8EJ,
part of Harcourt Education.
Raintree is a registered trademark of Harcourt Education Ltd.

Editorial: Nancy Dickmann and Louise Galpine
Design: Ron Kamen and Paul Davies and Associates
Illustrations: Nicholas Beresford-Davies
Picture Research: Peter Morris and Maria Joannou
Production: Séverine Ribierre

Originated by Dot Gradations
Printed and bound in China by South China Printing Company

ISBN 1 844 21046 4
07 06 05 04 03
10 9 8 7 6 5 4 3 2 1

British Library Cataloguing in Publication Data
Bingham, Jane
    World Art and Culture: Indian
    709.5'4
A full catalogue record for this book is available from the British Library.

Acknowledgements
The publishers would like to thank the following for permission to reproduce photographs: AKG p. **50**
(Jean Louis Nou); Alamy p. **33**; Alamy pp. **19** (Alan King), **32** (Robert Harding); Art archive pp. **21** (Musee
Guimet, Paris/ Dagli Orti), **8** (Victoria and Albert Museum/ Sally Chappell); Bridgeman Art Library pp. **51**
(Phillips, the International Fine Art Auctioneers, UK), **45** (Victoria & Albert Museum); Corbis pp. **22**
(Alison Wright), **6**, **9** (Angelo Hornak), **18** (Archivo Iconografico, S.A), **13** (Bennett Dean), **12** (Bob Krist),
16 (Charles & Josette Lenars), **7** (Charles Lenars), **49** (Chris Parker), **42** (David Cumming; Eye Ubiquitous),
15 (Galen Rowell), **36** (Gianni Baldizzone), **11**, **31** (Lindsay Hebberd), **41** (Michael Freeman), **44**
(Philadelphia Museum of Art), **35** (Ric Ergenbright), **43** (Sandro Vannini), **24** (Stapleton Collection);
Dinodia Picture Agency pp. **14**, **17**, **25** (Link); Edifice p. **39**; Getty Images/ Hulton p. **48**; Lebrecht
Collection p. **40** (inset); Panos Pictures pp. **46–47**; Panos pp. **5**, **26** (Jeremy Horner), **28** (Heldur Netocny),
29, **37** (Mark Henley), **23**, **27** (Sean Sprague).

Cover photograph of saris, reproduced with permission of Corbis/Lindsay Hebberd, and the head of a
statue with permission of The Bridgeman Art Library/National Museum of India, New Delhi, India.

The publishers would like to thank Dr. Crispin Branfoot for his assistance in the preparation of this book.

Contents

Words printed in the text in bold, **like this**, are explained in the Glossary.

Introduction

The vast country of India and its neighbours, Pakistan, Nepal, Bangladesh and Sri Lanka, are often known as the Indian subcontinent. Together, they form a triangle of land, or **peninsula**, that juts out into the sea. Within this peninsula, there are many different landscapes. Stretching across the north are the snow-covered Himalayas – the world's highest mountain range. In the north-west lies the barren Thar Desert, while the great Indus and Ganges Rivers run through very flat, fertile lands that are good for growing crops. In the centre of India is the high and rocky Deccan Plateau, with wooded hills running along its edges. Southern India and the island of Sri Lanka have tropical forests and long, sandy beaches.

Different ways of life

Over a billion people live in the Indian subcontinent, but their way of life varies enormously. In the high Himalayan mountains, farmers live in isolated mountain villages. Herders wander through the Thar Desert with their goats and camels. Farmers grow tea on the hills of southern India, while people on the coast earn their living by fishing. In some heavily forested areas, people still live in groups, with very little contact with the outside world.

This map of the Indian subcontinent shows the modern borders of India. However the culture of the Indian subcontinent spreads across contemporary borders and into India's neighbouring countries – Pakistan, Nepal, Bangladesh and Sri Lanka.

feet **HEIGHT** metres	
over 13120	over 4000
6560-13120	2000-4000
3277-6557	1000-1999
1640-3277	500-999
656-1637	200-499
under 656	under 200

4

Art is everywhere in India. Here, two women in colourful saris peer through a decorated doorway. One reason for the survival of so many traditional crafts in India is the influence of the great early 20th-century leader, Mahatma Gandhi. He believed passionately that village craftspeople would play a vital part in an independent India (see page 9).

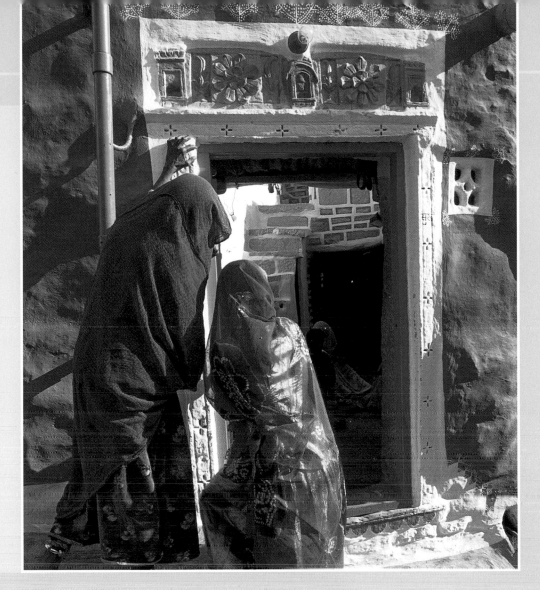

Nowadays, many Indians have moved to the cities, attracted by the hope of jobs, but around three-quarters of India's population still live in the country. Life in an Indian village continues in much the same way as it has done for hundreds of years, with people still practising traditional crafts.

Religions and beliefs

Religion plays a very important part in Indian life. Four major faiths – **Hinduism**, **Buddhism**, **Jainism** and **Sikhism** – all began in India. The Indian subcontinent also has one of the largest **Muslim** populations in the world. Each religion has its own buildings, festivals and ceremonies, and Indian artists often depict religious figures and stories.

Many forms of art

Everywhere in India, you can see colour and pattern – from women dressed in vivid fabrics and delicate jewellery, to houses and temples decorated inside and out. Each village has its own craft workers, and there are many rich traditions of music, poetry and dance.

This book explores different aspects of Indian art – such as carving, textiles and metalwork – and looks at individual works within these groupings. By looking at examples from many parts of the subcontinent, it aims to build up a picture of the richness and variety of Indian art.

An ancient civilization

The history of India stretches back over 5000 years. Farmers began to settle in the fertile Indus Valley before 3500 BCE, and gradually built cities and towns along the river banks. The ancient cities of Harappa and Mohenjo-daro were very well organized, with sewage systems, public baths and vast storehouses for grain. Each city had its own stone carvers and potters.

The Aryans arrive

The Indus Valley civilization lasted for over a thousand years, but around 1500 BCE tribes of people called **Aryans** began arriving in northern India. Gradually, they spread out all over the country, bringing a new way of life. The Aryans divided people into different groups according to their job. This way of grouping people was known as the **caste system** and it still survives in much of India. The Aryans also worshipped many gods and sang hymns to them. Many years later, the hymns were written down in holy books called the **Vedas**. These volumes formed the basis of the Hindu religion, the main faith in India today.

The birth of Buddhism

Ancient India was also the birthplace of the Buddhist religion. Around 500 BCE, an Indian prince called Siddhartha Gautama left his palace and began to live as a holy man. He became known as the Buddha and taught people to give up their possessions and to try to reach a state of peace, known as **nirvana**. Over the next 300 years, Buddhism spread throughout India, but it

This clay model of oxen pulling a water cart was made around 4000 years ago, by potters in the Indus Valley.

BCE | before 3500: farmers settle in the Indus Valley | 2500s: towns and cities built in the Indus Valley | 1500s: the Aryans arrive in India. Origins of Hindusim.

eventually became more popular in countries further east. Buddhists believe that you live many lives in different bodies. They spend a lot of their time meditating.

The rise of Jainism

About the same time as Buddhism was beginning to develop, another great preacher spread the religion of Jainism. The Jains built monasteries and temples all over India and their religion still has millions of followers there. Like Hindus, Jains worship many gods and goddesses. They believe that all violence is wrong, and that all forms of life are sacred – they even try to avoid harming insects.

Mauryans and Guptas

Around 320 BCE, a warrior called Chandragupta Maurya began to build up a large empire. The Mauryan Empire lasted for over 100 years and its most famous emperor was Asoka. During his reign, stone domes, called **stupas**, were built at places connected with the Buddha's life.

After the peaceful reign of Asoka, northern India was invaded several times, but in 320 CE a new family of emperors called the Guptas took control. The Gupta Empire is famous for its beautiful wall paintings and stone carvings. Classical Indian music and dance developed during this time, and the poet and playwright, Kalidasa, wrote about love and nature.

The graceful Buddhist cave paintings at Ajanta were painted during the Gupta dynasty, around the 6th century CE.

500s: birth of Buddhism and Jainism

321: the Mauryan Empire begins

185: the Mauryan Empire collapses

Sultans and Mughals

During the 700s, **Arab** armies from the north began invading India, and some Arabs settled there. Then, in 1206, a Turkish army general called Aibak declared himself Sultan of Delhi on the death of his leader, Muhammad of Ghur. The Sultans ruled northern India for the next 300 years, turning the Delhi region into a Muslim country and building forts, towers and **mosques**.

The Sultanate of northern India came to an end in 1526 when another group of Muslims – the **Mughals** – invaded India. This was the start of the great Mughal Empire, which lasted until 1857. Mughal emperors paid for beautiful palaces and mosques to be built. Poets, scholars, artists and musicians were all welcomed at their courts.

The British in India

From the 1500s onwards, European traders flocked to India to buy silk, spices, cotton and tea. They set up trading stations all over the country. By the 1800s the British East India Company controlled large areas of India. A year after the first Indian War of Independence in 1857, the British government seized control of the country, making India an important part of the British Empire.

The period when the British ruled India is known as the **Raj**. During the Raj, the British built schools, government buildings, churches and railways all over India. Many Indians learnt English, and British missionaries tried to persuade Indians to become Christians.

This painted wooden carving of an English soldier being eaten by a tiger was made by Indian craftsmen in the 18th century.

CE | 320: the Gupta Empire begins | c.535: the Gupta Empire ends | 711: Arab invasions begin. **Islam** introduced. | c.866: the Chola kingdom begins | 1206: the Sultanate of Delhi begins

Independence and afterwards

Eventually, the Indian people demanded the right to govern themselves. Following their inspiring leader, Mahatma Gandhi, they campaigned for an end to British rule. Finally, in 1947, India became independent. But India's Muslims and Hindus could not agree on their country's future. Consequently, the day before Independence, the mainly Muslim areas in the north formed the independent Muslim country of Pakistan. Pakistan was made up of two separate areas of land to the east and west of India. In 1971, after many years of war, East Pakistan became the new independent country of Bangladesh.

The subcontinent today

Today, parts of the Indian subcontinent suffer from flooding and droughts, some of its cities are very polluted, and many of its people are desperately poor. But despite all these problems, Indian village life continues to be peaceful. Although television and advertising have had an effect on people's lives, the main events of the year are still the sowing and harvesting of crops and the marking of the country's many religious festivals.

From the 800s to the 1500s powerful Hindu kingdoms flourished in southern India. The Chola kingdom was famous for its bronze statues, such as the one shown here, which depicts the Hindu god Krishna overpowering a snake demon.

1336: the kingdom of Vijayanagar begins

1526: the Mughal Empire begins

1600: the British East India Company is created

1858: the British government takes control of India

1947: Partition and Independence. British India splits into independent India and independent Pakistan.

Architecture

India has an astonishing range of buildings, including imposing forts, intricate **mosques** and lavish palaces. But many of its greatest buildings are temples – religious structures intended to fill the worshipper with awe and wonder. They were often built on a huge scale and covered with carvings.

Buddhist stupas

The first great temple builder was the Emperor Asoka, who ruled over most of the Indian subcontinent in the 3rd century BCE. Asoka built a series of huge stone burial mounds, known as **stupas**, in memory of the tomb of the Buddha. The most famous of these is at Sanchi in Madhya Pradesh. This massive monument is made up of a brick dome, covered in sandstone, and surrounded by a simple wall with four carved gateways. A circular walkway runs around the dome – used by monks for the sacred act of circumambulation (or 'walking around'). At the top of the dome is a stone copy of the umbrella which protected the raised Buddha from the Sun's harsh rays. **Buddhist** temple-builders all over India copied this basic shape for their stupas.

Temples at Ellora

Between the 7th and the 10th centuries CE, a remarkable set of temples was cut out of the steep, stone cliffs at Ellora in Maharashtra. These temples were built by Buddhists, **Hindus** and **Jains**, and for 200 years all three religions existed there peacefully side by side.

The earliest buildings at Ellora are Buddhist monasteries. Deep inside the cliff, tall stone galleries are filled with rows of pillars, each leading to a statue of the Buddha. These peaceful spaces were some of the last Buddhist monasteries to be built in India, before Hindus drove most of the Buddhists out of the country.

From 800 to 1000, Jain builders and sculptors created beautiful cave temples at Ellora. Elaborate altars were carved out of the cliff face and pillars were decorated with larger-than-life stone figures. But the most spectacular temple at Ellora was built by the Hindus. The colossal Kailasa temple, started around 760, is the largest stone structure in India. This gigantic open-air sculpture measures 33 metres (109 feet) wide by 50 metres (164 feet) long. The temple is covered with figures and animals and is meant to represent the city of the gods.

This exquisite Jain sculpture from the cave temples at Ellora shows Indrani, queen of the gods, seated on a lion beneath a mango wishing-tree.

Southern temples

The area around the Bay of Bengal has been called the 'cradle of Hindu architecture'. From here, styles of building and sculpture spread out all over India and into South-east Asia.

During the 7th century CE, the kings of the Pallava kingdom built an extraordinary group of temples at Mamallapuram, on the Bay of Bengal. Close to the shore are five surviving rectangular granite shrines. Each of the **shrines** has a domed roof supported by pillars, and is intended to represent a chariot of the gods. The stone shrines were probably copied from wooden carts that were used in religious processions.

Also at Mamallapuram is the famous Shore Temple, built on a rocky **promontory** sticking out into the sea. The temple has a roof shaped like a small pyramid, which rises in a series of tiers, growing smaller and smaller, until it ends in a miniature dome with a pointed spire.

Paradise mountain

The mountain-shaped roofs of Hindu temples are intended to represent the sacred Mount Meru. According to Hindu legends, Mount Meru is the paradise where the gods and goddesses have their homes.

These rock-cut *rathas* from Mamallapuram are part of a group of five temples, each named after a brother in the Hindu epic poem, the *Mahabharata*. Each of the *rathas* is carved in a different style.

The spectacular Sri Meenakshi temple in Madurai, southern India, has five towers, known as *gopuras*. The sides of the *gopuras* are encrusted with thousands of stucco figures from Hindu legends.

Kajuraho

The style of tiered and decorated building developed at Mamallapuram spread across India, growing richer and richer. By the 10th century CE, Hindu temples had become extremely elaborate. The Kandariya Mahadeo temple at Kajuraho is made up of a cluster of tall, tiered pinnacles – all of them covered in carvings. Inside the temple is an entrance hall, an assembly hall and a **sanctuary** containing a statue of Nataraja, god of the dance. The highest tower houses the sanctuary.

Later temples

By the 17th century, a new style of Hindu temple building had developed in southern India. High, wedge-shaped towers were smothered with colourful statues of gods and goddesses, animals and demons. These statues were made from **stucco** – a form of plaster – and painted in vivid colours. Most Hindu temples in India today are built in this **flamboyant** and dramatic style.

Mosques and minarets

The arrival of **Muslims** from the north had an enormous impact on India's architecture. In 1199, a Turkish soldier, Aibak, celebrated his victory in northern India by building a mosque, crowned by a huge **minaret**, or prayer tower. The minaret, which took over 150 years to build, is over 70 metres (229 feet) tall and for many years was the world's highest single tower. It had decorated balconies and was influenced by the architecture of Persia (present-day Iran).

Aibak was the first in a long line of Sultans of Delhi, and his successors built mosques, forts, palaces and tombs. Many of these buildings had pointed arches and tall, rounded domes copied from Persian architecture.

Mughal architecture

The **Mughal** Emperors ruled from 1526 to 1857, and left their stamp all over northern India. They built themselves elegant homes with shady courtyards and beautiful gardens, based on Persian palaces. The Mughals also built impressive, well-planned forts and spacious mosques with detailed minarets. The greatest of the Mughal builders was the Emperor Shah Jahan, who built the famous Taj Mahal.

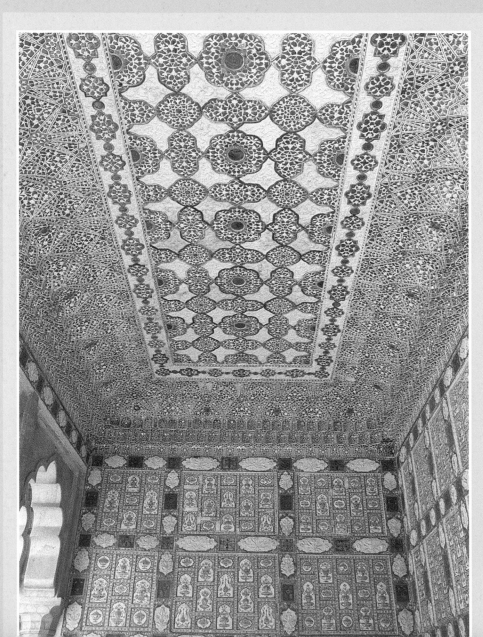

Maharajahs' palaces

During the 17th and 18th centuries, the powerful Hindu princes of Rajasthan, in north-west India, built splendid palaces. These palaces copied some of the features of Mughal architecture, such as large 'audience halls' for receiving guests and shady gardens with pools, but they were decorated in a much more extravagant style. The most elaborate of these palaces was built by **Maharajah** Jai Singh at Amber, in Rajasthan. It contained vast, glittering halls whose marble walls were **inlaid** with jewels and thousands of mirrors.

The glittering Shish Mahal (palace of mirrors) at Amber was built in the 1630s. The whole of the interior is covered with mirror mosaics and marble and decorated with carved and gilded plasterwork.

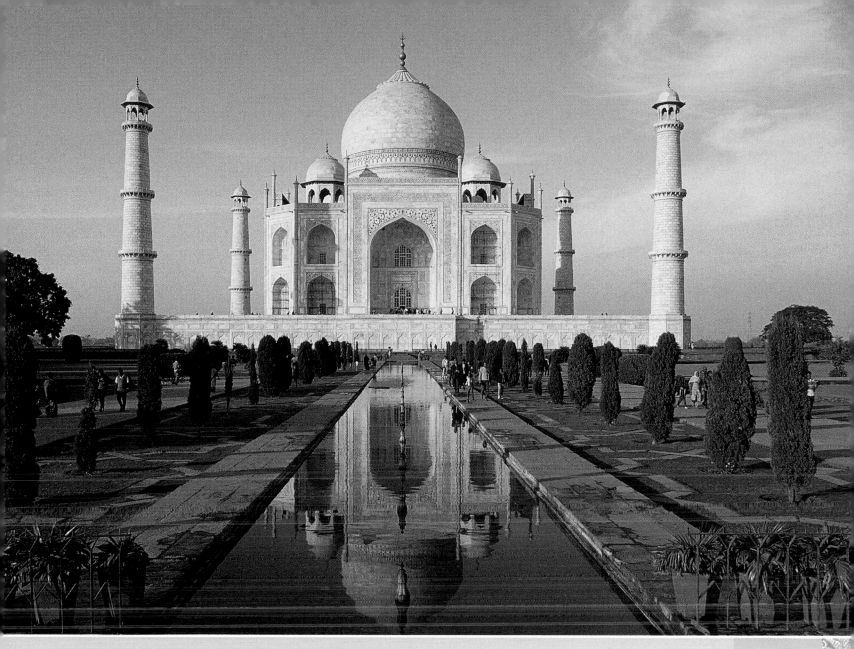

The white marble Taj Mahal is one of the world's most famous sights. Like many Mughal buildings, it is surrounded by beautiful gardens.

City buildings

The buildings in Indian cities are a great mixture of styles, from extravagant Hindu temples and elegant mosques, to modern skyscrapers and ramshackle slums. Traces of the British presence still exist in India's cities and towns. Many cities have government buildings, churches and railway stations, where the influence of British **Victorian** style is obvious.

Twin tombs

The Taj Mahal was built by Mughal Emperor Shah Jahan as a massive tomb, or **mausoleum**, for his beloved wife, Mumtaz Mahal. It took over 20 years to build and was completed in 1643. The Taj Mahal was constructed from carved white marble, and Shah Jahan planned a second mausoleum for himself made from black marble. But before he started work on the tomb his ambitious son seized power and threw his father into prison.

15

Wall painting and decoration

People in India have been painting and decorating the walls of their buildings for thousands of years. Some murals painted in temples show scenes of gods and legends, while wall decorations made for village homes tend to be simple but bold.

Paintings at Ajanta

Many early temples contained **frescoes**, but most of them have been lost. However, a stunning series of paintings survive from the 5th century CE in the **Buddhist** temple caves of Ajanta in Maharashtra. These skilful murals tell the story of the Buddha's many incarnations or lives. The figures are graceful and realistic, with lots of delicate detail in their clothing and headdresses.

Painted houses

In many parts of India, people paint the outsides of their houses with traditional patterns and designs. In Orissa, women from the Paraja group paint the walls of their mud-brick homes with bold **geometric** patterns in earth **pigments** – yellow **ochre**, orange ochre, black and white. In Gujarat, the outer walls of houses are decorated with patterns and symbols to prevent any evil from entering the house and to keep the people inside safe and well.

This painting from Ajanta shows the Buddha, Siddhartha Gautama, before he gave up his life as a prince and became a wandering holy man.

A dramatic painted ceiling in a bhunga house in Gujarat.

Special occasions

Often, walls are painted at different times of the year to celebrate festivals. These decorations can be simple handprints or elaborate designs. In Orissa, people paint intricate, white lacelike patterns onto the walls of their houses to celebrate the harvest festival.

Houses made from mud need regular resurfacing, and this work is often done at the time of a religious festival. The women of Madhya Pradesh apply a traditional wall decoration called *lipna* between the rice harvest and the planting of wheat. This is a time of thanksgiving and requests for a fruitful new crop. The decoration is made by first applying a layer of sticky mud and dung, mixed with black clay, and then adding a layer of whitewash. While the whitewash is still wet, finger marks are drawn through it, interweaving vertical, horizontal, diagonal and wavy lines.

◆ Raised patterns

The walls of traditional *bhunga* houses in Gujarat are decorated inside and out with raised geometric patterns moulded from mud and clay. These patterns are sometimes painted in different colours but are often simply covered with whitewash. Sometimes, pieces of mirror are set into the designs, which are similar to patterns found in the embroidery of the region. Girls learn the traditional geometric patterns from their mothers, and each pattern has its own name.

Stone carving

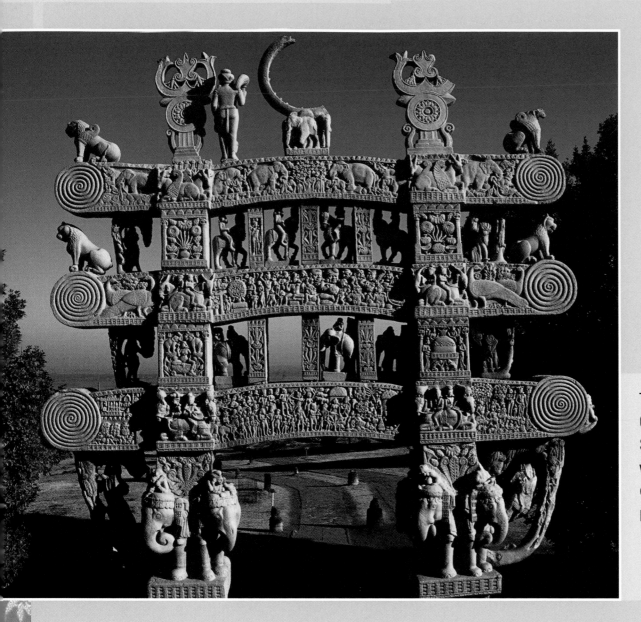

The gates of the Great Stupa at Sanchi are covered with incredibly elaborate carvings of people and animals.

As early as 2600 BCE, stoneworkers in the Indus Valley were carving large figures and small stone seals. The figures may have represented rulers or gods, while the seals, which were **engraved** with animals and letters, were probably used by merchants to label their goods.

The most famous early stone monuments are the polished sandstone pillars set up by the Emperor Asoka in the 3rd century BCE. These tall columns had Asoka's laws engraved on them and most of them were topped with carved animal **capitals**.

Because the animals are carved with great skill and attention to detail, they appear remarkably realistic.

Carvings on temples

The tradition of covering temples with carvings began very early. The gates of the **Buddhist stupas** at Sanchi, begun in the 1st century BCE, show lively, crowded scenes from the life of the Buddha. This type of carving, when figures emerge from the surface of the stone is known as **relief**.

By the 5th century, Buddhist, **Jain** and **Hindu** sculptors were carving relief scenes on the walls of their temples, but also making small, free-standing sculptures, as well as towering figures attached to pillars. The Jains were especially famous for their graceful depictions of the human body.

Perhaps the most famous sculptures in India are the figures decorating the Kajuraho temples in Madhya Pradesh. These temples, which were built in the 11th century, are dedicated to the gods Shiva, Vishnu and Surya. The carvings on their walls show gods and goddesses dancing, kissing and embracing each other.

Statues of the Buddha

India's stone carvers have produced many beautiful statues of the Buddha. During the time of the Gupta emperors, Buddhist sculptors at Mathura in Uttar Pradesh created a series of large-scale statues carved from sandstone. They show the Buddha looking serene with a slight smile on his face and his eyes half closed in **meditation**.

Stone carving today

The ancient traditions of stone carving are still continued in India today, as families pass down traditional practices from one generation to the next. Sculptors still make small-scale statues of gods and goddesses, which are used by Indians in their worship but also bought by tourists. Each region has its own different materials, such as soft red sandstone in Rajasthan, polished black stone in Bihar and granite in Tamil Nadu.

This vast statue of the reclining Buddha is 14 metres long and was carved out of rock in Sri Lanka in the 12th century CE. The Buddha is often shown with serene, **stylized** features.

Metalwork and jewellery

India's metalworkers have a vast range of skills. Using iron, brass, copper and tin, village blacksmiths make tools, pans and cooking implements. Workers skilled in bronze produce religious statues, while goldsmiths and silversmiths create exquisite jewellery. There is also a long tradition of combining metal with enamel to make decorative vases, daggers and jewellery. This type of metalwork **inlaid** with enamel is known as *bidri*.

Enamel work

The metalworkers of Jaipur are famous for their *meenakari* work. This is a type of **enamelling** in which patterns are hollowed out of silver or gold, filled with enamel, and then fired in a furnace. The patterns usually show flowers and are coloured in red, green and blue. *Meenakari* work is used for earrings and necklaces, but also to make decorative boxes and vases.

Statues from bronze

As early as the 2nd millennium BCE, people in India knew how to cast objects from bronze, using the demanding lost wax process (see box below). The earliest known figure in bronze comes from the ancient city of Mohenjo-daro in the Indus Valley and shows a dancing girl. Between the 10th and 13th centuries, metalworkers from the Chola kingdom in southern India produced statues of gods and goddesses in graceful poses. Although their headdresses and clothing are very detailed, the faces of the statues are simple and **stylized**.

◈ The lost wax process

The lost wax process is a complicated technique, which requires great patience and skill. First, a rough model of the final sculpture is made in clay. This is known as the core. Then a layer of beeswax is applied over the clay core. The beeswax is carefully moulded into shape, and extra strips of decoration are added using a moulding stick. When the beeswax model is finished, it is covered with three layers of clay, to form a clay mould, with a hole in its base so the wax can run out. The clay mould is then fired, and the wax melts away. Molten (liquid) bronze is poured into the empty mould and left to cool. Once the metal is completely cool, the clay mould is broken open and the metal sculpture can be taken out and polished. Only at this final stage, does the sculptor know if the process has been a success.

Statues today

Metalworkers in India today still make statues of gods and goddesses, following rules laid down in religious texts. These texts describe the exact proportions, materials and techniques for making images. In southern India, bronze statues are believed to absorb the energy of gods and are stored in the **inner sanctum** (the holiest part) of the temple.

This bronze statue was made in the Chola kingdom. It shows the dance of the Hindu god Nataraja, known as 'the destroyer'.

Jewellery

Jewellery is a very important part of Indian dress and culture, and Indian women usually wear more jewellery than Western women do. The earliest surviving statues from India show women adorned with necklaces, bracelets and anklets. In India, jewellery can be a sign of wealth and status, but it can also have symbolic value. For example, some people believe that gold symbolizes life and purity.

Different types

Each part of India has its own style of jewellery. In Jaipur, women wear ornaments set with gemstones, a technique known as *kundan*, while the women of Hyderabad make exquisite pearl jewellery. Orissa is a major centre for silver **filigree** work, which involves making a lacy trellis with twisted silver wire. Rajasthani girls and women wear heavy silver jewellery. Delicate gold necklaces and bracelets are made in the south.

This young bride from the city of Varanasi in northern India is adorned with gold and pearls for her wedding celebrations.

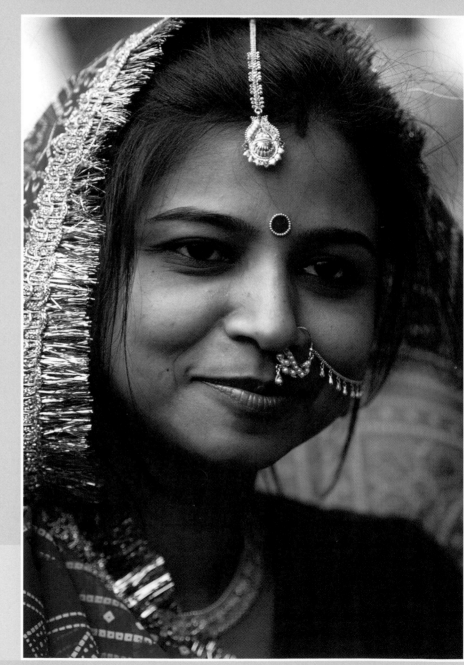

❖ The language of gemstones

Some Indians believe that the movements of the planets have an effect on human lives. Each of the major gemstones is seen as a symbol of a different planet.

ruby:	Sun
topaz:	Jupiter
pearl:	Moon
diamond:	Venus
emerald:	Mercury
sapphire:	Saturn
coral:	Mars

Rajasthani women and girls wear masses of heavy silver jewellery as a sign of their wealth and status.

Weddings and wealth

On her wedding day, an Indian woman is covered in beautiful gold and jewels. Traditionally, the only wealth that a woman has is her jewellery, so a bride will be given many presents of jewels by her family and in-laws before her wedding day.

In Rajasthan, the amount of jewellery a woman wears varies according to her wealth. She may wear a *tikka* or circular pendant on her forehead, dangling earrings, a choker round her neck, a nosering, a girdle around her waist, a series of bracelets and a set of anklets with tiny bells on them. Finally, if she is married, she will also wear *chakti* or toe rings. Not to be outdone, Rajasthani men commonly wear chokers, earrings and bracelets, too.

23

Painting

During the 10th century, artists in India began to produce illustrated books - holy texts accompanied by miniature paintings. The first illustrated books were **Buddhist** texts painted on palm leaves and bound between wooden covers. Later, **Jain** artists illustrated their sacred texts with lively scenes. The early Jain painters used mainly red and blue **pigments**, highlighted with gold. They often showed their figures in **profile**, but with two eyes - the far eye was shown sticking out beyond the figure's nose!

Mughal miniatures

The **Mughal** Empire was the great age of miniature painting. Emperors **commissioned** artists to paint delightful scenes. Mughal miniatures began as book illustrations and they are usually book-sized. They are delicately coloured and full of detail. They often show life at court, hunting scenes and animals. Although the Mughals were Muslims, they also encouraged **Hindu** painters, who produced lively illustrations of Hindu legends. Stories of the blue-skinned god, Krishna, were especially popular.

In the 18th century, the Hindu **maharajas** of Rajasthan encouraged the art of miniature painting. Rajasthani paintings tend to be bolder than Mughal miniatures and to use brighter colours.

An 18th-century Mughal miniature showing four women in a garden pavilion. Mughal miniatures are famous for their clear colours and delicate brushwork.

24

A Tanjore painting of a goddess and her handmaidens, shown in typically bold and dramatic style

◈ Miniature painting

During the Mughal period, artists painted miniatures on paper made from silk, cotton, bamboo or **jute**. After polishing the paper's surface with a ball of agate (a semi-precious stone), they sketched in their design with a fine brush made from squirrel hair. The design was then covered with a thin layer of white and the artists went over the details with a black line before applying the colour. Paints were usually made from **minerals** found in the earth. They included the very rare ultramarine (an intense pure blue) and silver and gold leaf. Last of all, extra details, such as faces were painted in. For really detailed work, the miniature artists used brushes made from a single baby squirrel hair!

Tanjore paintings

In Tanjore in southern India, artists produce dramatic, glittering paintings of gods and goddesses. Details from the painting, such as headdresses and jewellery, are moulded in plaster so that they stand out slightly from its surface. Then they are painted with gold and silver leaf and **inlaid** with pieces of coloured glass and semi-precious stones. Tanjore painting began in the 18th century and its artists were influenced by Western styles of art. Artists use vivid, almost luminous colours because their paintings were originally kept inside darkened rooms or temples, where they needed to stand out.

People in India have been weaving and decorating cloth for thousands of years. Fragments of printed cloth survive from the ancient city of Mohenjo-daro, providing evidence that Indian cloth makers were using dyes at least 2000 years before the Europeans. When European traders arrived in India in the 15th century, they were amazed by the range of dazzling coloured cloth that they found there, as well as by the skilful techniques of printing and embroidery used by Indian textile makers.

Many types

Each region of the Indian subcontinent has its own traditions for textile-making. In the desert regions of the north-west, women dye cotton brilliant colours and cover it with intricate embroidery. Weavers in Bengal make silks and muslin (a type of soft, filmy cotton). Painted cloth, known as chintz, comes from the east, and Kashmir is famous for its woollen embroidered shawls.

Using dyes

Until the late 19th century, cloth makers in India dyed their wool, cotton or silk using natural **pigments** made from **minerals**, such as red **ochre**, or from plants. The madder plant produced a deep scarlet; indigo made a deep, inky blue; and turmeric created a golden yellow. Nowadays, most cloth makers in India use chemical dyes, but they still use traditional colours.

Dyed saris drying in the sun, in Rajasthan.

These embroidered hangings from Rajasthan show the incredible range of colours and patterns produced by the local women. Rajasthani clothing is equally colourful and is often inset with mirrors that sparkle in the sunlight.

Embroideries from Rajasthan

The north-western state of Rajasthan is famous for its embroidered cloth. Before a young woman gets married, she and her family work for several years to prepare a **dowry** of embroideries that she will take with her to her new home. The embroidered items include a costume for the bride and groom, hangings for their house and **trappings** for their animals. All the items are embroidered with traditional patterns, and passed down from mother to daughter. The designs often include small, glittering mirrors and are inspired by local plants and animals.

◇ The language of colour

Colours often have a special significance in Indian traditional dress. Red symbolizes love, indigo is the colour of the gods and pale blue represents the sky. Saffron is the colour of the earth, but also of poets and yogi (holy men).

Block printing

Block printing is a quick and inexpensive way of decorating cloth. It is often used to make **saris**, *dhotis* (cloths worn by many Indian men) and floor spreads. Block printers use small wooden blocks with patterns carved on them. The blocks can be used in two ways. Either they are coated with dye and stamped onto a cloth, or they are covered with '**resist**' – a material such as mud, gum or wax – which resists the effect of a dye. When the cloth is dyed, the areas covered with resist remain unchanged.

Block-printed cloths have simple, repeated patterns and usually only a few colours. In western India, intricate block-printed geometric designs of flowers are common, showing the influence of **Mughal** art.

Tie-dye printing

The tie-dye method of printing cloth is used in many parts of Asia and Africa, but Indian cloth makers use the technique in a very distinctive way. Indian tie-dye fabrics are usually covered with hundreds of tiny circles of colour, produced by tying off minute areas of cloth before it is dyed. These brilliant dots of colour are arranged in **geometric** patterns and can look very dramatic – especially in the combinations of yellow, white and red often seen in Rajasthan.

This man is using a printing block to decorate cotton cloth. The same pattern is printed many times to create the total design.

Tie-dyed cloth can be produced in huge quantities. Here, mounds of dyed cotton are waiting to be washed.

◈ Tie-dye

Making a tie-dyed fabric with several different colours is a long process.

1. First, the pattern is marked on a cloth with a paint that will later wash out.

2. Then all the areas to be tied are pinched together and tied tightly with string. The fabric is dyed for the first time, with yellow or another light colour, leaving the tied areas white.

3. Once the cloth has been rinsed, squeezed and dried, it is tied again in a pattern that will later appear as yellow dots. Then it is dyed in a darker colour, such as red or green.

4. If other still darker colours are needed, the cloth is tied a third time to form a pattern of red or green dots. Then it is dyed once more with black, brown or dark red.

5. After the final dyeing, all the knots are untied and the cloth is washed several times.

Painting on cloth

In the eastern state of Andhra Pradesh, there is a long tradition of cloth painting, known as *kalamkari*. These large-scale paintings usually show gods and goddesses or mythical creatures surrounded by a decorative border. Traditionally, textile artists used pens to draw their designs on large sheets of cotton, then painted in the colours. The artists used special colours for different characters: gods were blue, women were yellow and bad characters or demons were red. However, over the last 20 years, the production of most *kalamkari* has been simplified – fewer colours are used and the coloured areas are printed using blocks, instead of being filled in by hand.

Appliqué work

Appliqué is the technique of stitching cut-out designs on to a larger piece of cloth. It is used in western India to make large **canopies**, hangings and animal trappings to be used in celebrations. Appliqué work was probably introduced into India by Western traders. Appliqué hangings and canopies often show simplified humans and animals, such as elephants and peacocks, surrounded by a patterned border.

Kashmir shawls

Kashmir shawls are woven from very fine **pashmina** wool, which comes from a special type of mountain goat. These goats live in China and Tibet, but their wool is bought by Indian merchants to be woven in Kashmir.

Traditional Kashmir shawls have colourful patterned borders which are woven on a loom. This is very time-consuming work and nowadays the decoration is usually added by embroiderers. Kashmir shawls were very popular in Europe from the 1800s onwards, but by the beginning of the 20th century demand for them had slumped. However, in recent years, pashminas have become fashionable. They are much simpler to make than traditional Kashmir shawls and have helped to revive the weaving industry in Kashmir.

Varanasi brocades

Brocades are rich fabrics woven with warp (lengthways) and weft (widthways) threads of different colours and often of different materials. Varanasi brocades are woven in silk, often decorated with a raised pattern of gold and silver threads, especially on the borders. The Varanasi weavers work on large looms, with many strings, and need to be extremely skilled to work out the complicated patterns. These specialist workers are not given the usual name of 'weavers' but are known as 'artists' instead. Their brocades are often made into wedding robes for wealthy brides.

This rich brocade from Varanasi is interwoven with silver threads and has an elaborate pattern of flowers and peacocks.

Ceramics

Throughout the Indian countryside, raw clay and **earthenware** (another name for clay fired at a low temperature) play a vital part in everyday life. Houses are made from clay bricks and often covered with tiles made from **terracotta** (an orangey-red clay). Grain is stored in large containers made from unfired clay, and cooking stoves are also made from unbaked clay. A whole range of cooking and storage pots is made from earthenware. Clay pots are used to carry water and cattle are fed and watered from large clay mangers set into the ground. Terracotta dishes and offerings play an important part in religious ceremonies.

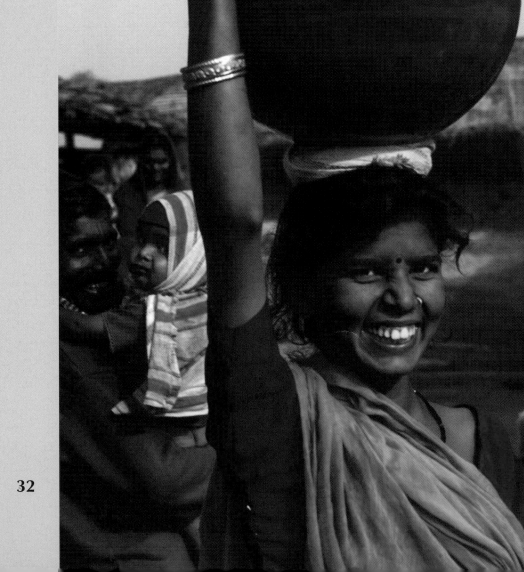

A Rajasthani woman carries a simple terracotta water pot on her head. Unglazed pots like this have been made in India for thousands of years.

An ancient craft

Fragments of pots have been found in India dating back over 8000 years. By 2550 BCE skilful potters from the Indus Valley were making pots, bowls and figures of mother goddesses. They also created a variety of terracotta toys, from dolls and animals with moving parts to whistles in the shape of birds.

During the Mauryan Empire, potters made highly polished black pots, while the Gupta period is famous for its bricks, tiles and pots that were decorated by painting, stamping and **incising** patterns in clay. The **Mughal** emperors introduced a new kind of ceramic ware – urns, plates and dishes painted with colourful patterns, which were protected by a glaze. But these items were made for the court, so the sophisticated style of the Mughal potters did not spread to the villages.

Using pots

Most Indian villagers use simple earthenware pots that have been fired at a low temperature and left unglazed. This kind of earthenware is especially useful for storing water, as it keeps the water cool by allowing some liquid to **evaporate** through the sides of the pot. Pots used for eating and storing food are frequently replaced. Containers used for tea, milk and yoghurt are often thrown away and broken after only one use. It is common for all household pottery to be replaced at festivals and at special occasions, such as births, marriages and deaths.

This fragment of Gupta period sculpture shows a young couple. It dates from the 4th or 5th century CE, and was found in Bihar.

◈ Kachcha and pakka

Clay in its unfired state is called *kachcha*, which means uncooked or impure. Once it is fired, it becomes *pakka*, which means cooked or pure. These two words are commonly used by Indians to describe things that are bad or polluted (*kachcha*) or good and well made (*pakka*). The English word, 'pukka' comes from *pakka*.

Village potters

Most Indian villages have their own potters, who live together away from the centre of the village. The potters always come from the same family, and traditional shapes and decorations are passed from one generation of relatives to the next. Each region of India has its own distinctive traditions.

Everyday pots

In Himachal Pradesh, in the high Himalayas, potters make a range of rounded pots and bowls for cooking, storing and eating food. They also make some special ceremonial dishes to be used for marriages, weddings and funerals. Most of the pots are made from terracotta, and are decorated using white and black **slip** (a kind of clay paint). The pots are painted with rippling lines, closely-spaced diagonal lines, **geometric** designs and dots. The designs are often based on animals, leaves and flowers.

Decorative pots

In the state of Uttar Pradesh, some potters produce elegant vases, incense burners and plates to be sold in towns. These pots are black and glossy and are **inlaid** with silver designs. After the pots have been shaped, they are coated with a slip made from clay, tree bark and leaves mixed with **soda** collected from a local lake – a mixture that turns black when the pot is fired. Then the pots are covered with mustard oil and polished with a soft cloth to make them shine. After this, they are ready to be **engraved** with delicate patterns, using a sharp metal spike. Once the pots have been fired, a mixture of lead, zinc and mercury is pressed by hand into the engraved lines to make the silver designs. The patterns, which often feature flowers, have been the same for hundreds of years, and were influenced by Mughal art.

◈ Making pots

To make the rounded pots produced in Himachal Pradesh, potters first use a wheel to make the basic shape. After this, the pot's thick walls are beaten until the pot stretches to almost twice its original size. The potter moistens the clay of the pot and holds a large rounded stone inside it while beating the outside with a curved wooden paddle. Often a pot is beaten three times, each time using a lighter paddle. After they have been decorated, pots are piled up in large, open **kilns** (ovens) in very large quantities. Sometimes, as many as a thousand pots are fired together.

A village potter at work in Rajasthan. Nowadays, most Indian pots are made on a wheel and finished off by hand.

Religious offerings

Many potters in India make terracotta objects, which **Hindus** give as **votive offerings** to their gods. The offerings are placed in temples and shrines, either to ask the gods for a favour or to give thanks for a blessing. For example, a farmer who hopes his cattle will produce good milk will offer a clay buffalo, while a woman with a bad leg will give a model leg. Votive offerings can take many forms, including animals and human figures, houses, carts and even musical instruments.

Offerings to Aiyanar

In the southern state of Tamil Nadu, life-sized terracotta statues of humans and animals line paths leading to the shrines of the Hindu god, Aiyanar. Horses are shown wearing saddles and bridles, ready to carry Aiyanar's spirit soldiers out into the villages at night so that they can protect the people from evil. These elaborate sculptures have been made for hundreds of years. Nowadays, the clay sculptures are often painted in vivid colours.

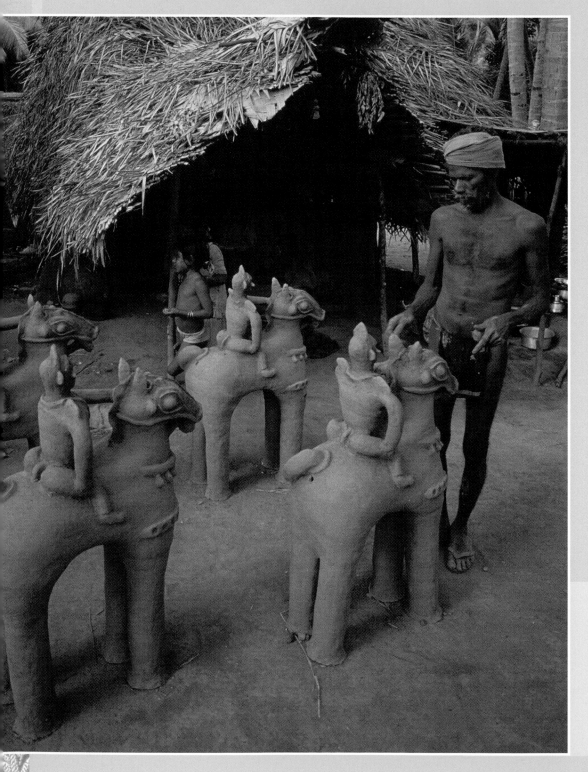

A potter from Tamil Nadu adds the final details to a set of terracotta horses. The horses will be brightly painted and glazed before they are fired in a kiln.

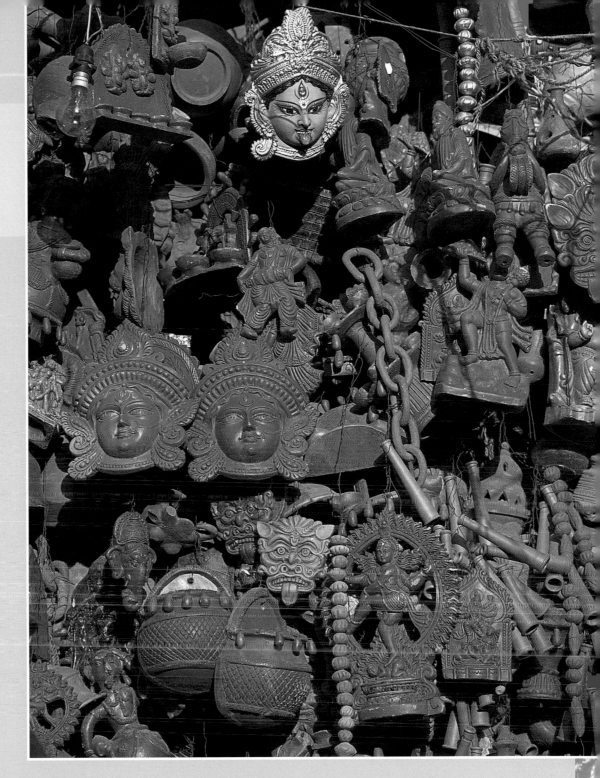

An amazing collection of terracotta votive offerings covers the walls of a shrine in northern India.

Plaques from Rajasthan

In the north-western state of Rajasthan, there is a tradition of making terracotta plaques – upright plates that are decorated with painted figures of gods. Once a year during January, Hindus make a **pilgrimage** by bus and on foot, sometimes for hundreds of miles, to the village of Molela to buy these plaques. A priest helps the pilgrims to choose the gods appropriate to their own lives and then leads a procession to a nearby river. Here, the gods are worshipped before being taken home and placed in household shrines.

Temples and jhars

The town of Vishnupur in West Bengal is famous for its terracotta temples. From the 16th to the 19th century, people built stone temples that were covered with ornate terracotta tiles showing scenes from the great Hindu epic poems, the **Ramayana** and the **Mahabharata**.

Today's descendants of these artists produce a range of votive objects in clay, including horses, tigers, elephants and snakes, as well as toys and pots. They also make terracotta sculptures known as *jhars* to be placed in shrines. A *jhar* is shaped rather like a miniature bush, decorated with figures of gods. It stands on a circular base, like the stem of a bush in the ground.

37

Wood carving

Wood is used in India in the home and in worship. Village woodworkers produce bowls, spoons, chests, trays, and furniture for everyday use. Traditional woodcarvers make religious statues, following instructions laid down hundreds of years ago in holy books. Skilled workers specialize in luxury items, such as carved wooden chests and statuettes, while carpenters build wooden houses with carved door frames, window frames and balconies.

Different woods

There is a huge variety of wood to choose from in India. In Kashmir, trays and fruit bowls are made from polished walnut wood. Ebony and rosewood are carved into delicate boxes in Uttar Pradesh. The red sandalwood of Andhra Pradesh is traditionally used to carve figures of gods and dolls, while craft workers in Orissa make **lacquered** boxes from the stalks of the bamboo plant.

Inlaid wood

Northern India is famous for its chests, trays and tables made from wood **inlaid** with mother-of-pearl, ivory, tortoiseshell, horn or silver. The demanding art of inlaying wood was first introduced to India in the 13th century by the Sultans of Delhi, and techniques of inlay were perfected at the court of the **Mughals**. Skilled craftsmen carve intricate patterns into soft wood, and then fill these patterns with different materials. Today, the tradition of inlaying wood continues in Gujarat, Rajasthan and Delhi, but ivory inlay has now been largely replaced by plastic. This change in artists' materials reflects the increased awareness in Indian culture of the need to preserve endangered elephants.

Wooden homes

Carpenters in India build houses in a range of styles. Perhaps the most elaborate wooden buildings in India are the *haveli* houses of Gujarat with their overhanging, carved balconies and decorated windows and doorways. The elegant *tharavad* homes of Kerala are brilliant pieces of architecture in deep brown teakwood. The woodworkers of Uttar Pradesh are famous for their delicate **fretwork** screens, influenced by Mughal palaces.

Inside many Indian homes are wooden tables, chairs, chests and beds. These pieces of furniture may be simple and basic, but they can also be very delicately carved. For example, the woodworkers of Jodhpur, in Rajasthan, produce beautifully carved chairs with woven rope seats and exquisite latticework on their backrests. In some parts of India, carpenters make full-sized, painted swings to hang from beams inside houses.

A row of wooden mansions in Sidhpur built by a sect of Shi'a Muslims prominent in the city between 1539 and 1589 CE.

◈ Carpenters' chariots

In ancient India, carpenters were highly respected. According to some historical accounts, village carpenters sometimes had their own wooden chariots, which they made themselves, and drove through their villages with great pride.

Music plays an important part in Indian life. Ancient hymns are chanted at **Hindu** ceremonies. Travelling musicians wander from village to village, playing tambourines, pipes, drums and flutes, and singing traditional folk songs. Classical Indian musicians hold concerts in cities and towns. The instruments used by classical and folk musicians are made by skilled craft workers, who follow designs that have stayed the same for hundreds of years.

Classical music

Indian classical music is divided into two main branches: **Hindustani music** in the north and **Karnataka music** in the south. Musicians from the north and south use different musical instruments. Both Hindustani and Karnataka music are based on a combination of **raga**, which means melody, and **taal**, which is rhythm. *Ragas* can be sung, but also played on a stringed instrument, such as the **sitar**. *Taal* is provided by drums.

Musical instruments

The sitar is the most important instrument in Hindustani music. It usually has seven main strings, which run all the way along the instrument, and about ten 'sympathetic strings' inside its long, hollow neck. When the main strings are played, the sympathetic strings vibrate as well, creating a rippling sound.

Another stringed instrument, the *veena*, is played by Karnataka musicians. It is made from a hollow bamboo tube with seven strings stretched over it, attached to two hollow gourds. The gourds act as sound boxes, magnifiying the sound of the strings.

The veena is one of the country's most ancient stringed instruments, and originates from South India.

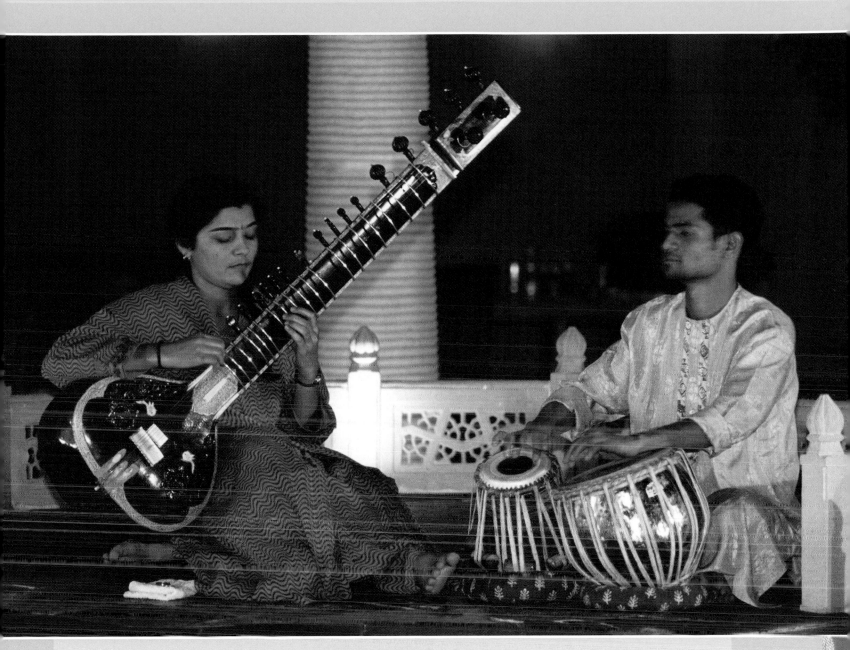

A sitar player is accompanied by a drummer on a tabla. The small drum on the right, known as a *dayan*, plays the higher notes.

Tabla is the name for a pair of hand drums that provide the rhythm in Hindustani classical music. A tabla consists of a small right-hand drum, called a *dayan*, and a larger left-hand one, called a *bayan*. The *dayan* produces the higher notes, while the metal *bayan* plays the lower notes. Both drums have a leather skin stretched over them, held by straps which can be tightened or loosened to alter the sound. Each drumskin has a large black spot made from a mixture of gum, soot and iron filings. This mixture produces a strong, almost bell-like sound when it is hit.

41

Dance, theatre and cinema

In India, the ancient art of dancing is closely linked to the **Hindu** religion. There are five main forms of classical dance and they all tell stories from ancient legends and **epics**. Each dance form comes from a different region and has its own style and costumes.

Bharata Natyam and Kathakali

The oldest form of dance is *Bharata Natyam*, which comes from the southern state of Tamil Nadu. It is described in a text called *Natya Shastra*, which was written between 200 BCE and 200 CE. *Bharata Natyam* dancers combine strength and grace and use hand gestures to tell a story. The dramatic dance form of *Kathakali* comes from Kerala, also in the south. *Kathakali* dancers wear elaborate costumes and play different characters. Only men can become *Kathakali* dancers. They have to train for many years before they can perform the energetic dances, which often continue throughout the night.

Changing faces

Kathakali dancers wear dramatic face paint to represent different characters. The colour of the paint depends on the character being played. Black is the colour for villains and green is for heroes. The paint takes several hours to apply. Finally, small seeds are placed in the dancers' eyes to colour the whites of their eyes red.

This Kathakali dancer is playing the part of a hero. Dancers need to be incredibly fit to perform for hours, wearing full make-up and heavy headdresses.

Odissi, Manipuri and Kathak

Odissi is a gentle dance form which began in the temples of Orissa in the east. *Odissi* dancers move gracefully, with small, precise hand gestures. *Manipuri* dancers from the north-east wear highly-coloured costumes and perform gentle, swaying movements, creating a hypnotic effect.

Kathak is a **Muslim** dance form from northern India. It began during the **Mughal** Empire, when dancers often performed for rulers in their palaces. *Kathak* dance is fast and exciting, with rapid foot stamping and spins.

Theatre

In India's big cities, plays are performed in theatres, but travelling actors visit small towns and villages to stage traditional dramas. Puppet shows are also very popular in the country. The most famous Indian playwright was Kalidasa, who wrote in the late 4th century CE to the early 5th century CE. His plays on the themes of love and magic are still frequently performed today.

Cinema

The film business is booming in India, with around 800 new films being released every year. Indian films usually have a dramatic story line, involving plenty of romance, but also fighting, singing and dancing. The main centre for Indian film-making is based in the city of Mumbai (which used to be called Bombay) and is known as Bollywood.

Like the films they advertize, Indian movie posters are very colourful and dramatic. Bollywood films are now becoming popular outside India.

Stories and writing

Storytelling is very important in Indian culture. For centuries, folk tales and religious legends were passed down from generation to generation as people memorized stories and told them aloud. The two most famous collections of stories are the long **Hindu** poems, the **Mahabharata** and the **Ramayana**. Written in the ancient language of **Sanskrit**, these two **epics** tell legends of the Hindu gods and the early history of the Indian people.

The *Mahabharata* was written down around 300 BCE. It is set on the Ganges plain and tells the fortunes of two rival families. The poem contains the **Bhagavad Gita**, or 'The Song of God', the most important text in the Hindu religion. The *Ramayana* was written down some time between the 2nd and 4th century BCE. It tells the story of the Hindu god Rama and his wife Sita, who follow the virtuous path through life, known as the *dharma*.

Both the *Mahabharata* and the *Ramayana* have had a huge impact on Indian art. Even today, artists paint characters and scenes from the poems, while many Indian films and plays are based on their stories.

Scrolls

In Bengal, artist-performers, known as *patua*, make paintings on scrolls and carry them from village to village, telling stories from legends and using the pictures to illustrate their tales. One kind of *patua* painting is complete in all its detail except that the **iris** in the central figure's eye is missing. When someone dies, the artist visits the dead person's house with a painting that is supposed to represent him. The artist tells the relatives that the dead man's soul is wandering, not knowing where to go. When the artist paints in the iris, the dead man's soul can find its way to paradise.

This story painting was made by a member of the patua caste around 1880. It shows the monkey king Hanuman revealing that the gods Rama and Sita are living in his heart.

This illustration from the Hindu poem, the *Ramayana*, shows the Monkey King sending out messengers to search for the goddess, Sita. Many Hindu book illustrations use vivid colours and show dramatic landscapes.

Beautiful books

India has a long tradition of beautifully written and illustrated texts. In the 16th century, the **Mughals** introduced the art of calligraphy – very fine writing done with special pens. During the Mughal Empire, **Muslim** scribes used beautiful calligraphy to write out the Qur'an, the holy book of **Islam**. They also wrote chronicles about the lives of the emperors and even created recipe books. At the same time, Hindu artists were producing colourful illustrated books, telling the stories of their gods and goddesses.

◈ Story boxes

Sometimes, stories are told through a series of pictures painted in a story box. The box, known as a *kavad*, is shaped like a man – the storyteller. As the story box is opened up, more and more scenes from the story are revealed.

Many crafts

The Indian subcontinent is full of craft workers. Most of them work at home in their villages, but some have small workshops in cities. Families pass on these skills from one generation to the next, keeping the crafts alive in Indian regional cultures.

Leatherwork

Almost every Indian village has a cobbler who makes leather bags, saddles and sandals, known as *chappals*. In the cities, leatherworkers often create more elaborate items, such as pointed slippers with elaborate fabric decorations stitched on to them. Leather workers in the Punjab create **appliqué** patterns by stitching coloured leather pieces on to an undyed leather base. Skilled craft workers in Madhya Pradesh embroider red leather with gold and silk thread. In the desert regions of the north-west, lamps and lampshades are made from camel hides, which are then coloured and decorated and finally plated with thin gold leaf.

Papier mâché

In Kashmir, in northern India, people make beautifully decorated trays, boxes and other small objects from papier mâché. First, the objects are moulded from a mixture of wet paper and glue. Then they are covered all over with painted designs of flowers, birds and animals. The fine details are painted using a single goat's hair. Finally, a layer of varnish is applied, making the objects stronger and giving them an attractive, shiny surface.

Carpets

Carpets and rugs are made in many areas of India, but the most famous are the intricately patterned carpets of Kashmir. The Kashmiri weavers make their carpets on a loom, knotting all the threads by hand. The weavers always leave a single, deliberate mistake in their weaving. This is done as a mark of respect to Allah, because **Muslims** believe that only He is capable of perfection.

Toys and puppets

In many parts of India, woodcarvers make toys, dolls and puppets. Usually, carvers follow traditional designs for animals and people, but they also create models of modern objects, such as planes and cars. The toys and dolls are painted in vivid colours and are often decorated with fabric.

Street art

The cities of the Indian subcontinent are full of colour.
Gigantic posters for the latest films line the streets. Trucks,
vans and buses are often covered with hand-painted
decorations, while rickshaws (open-air taxis pedalled by a
driver) may have colourful fabric hoods with ribbons and
ornaments hanging from them. During religious festivals in
Rajasthan, carts with embroidered canopies are pulled
through the streets.

In Old Dehli, a
confusing range of
street signs compete
with an outsized
movie poster for
people's attention.

Cross-currents

During the course of India's long history, many different peoples arrived in the country and left their mark on its art and culture. In their turn, Indian arts and crafts have had a dramatic impact on the rest of the world.

The impact of the Arabs

The people with the strongest influence on Indian art were the **Arabs**. From the 700s onwards, **Muslim** Arabs from the north began to arrive in India, bringing a new religion, new styles of building and a different way of life. The **Mughals**, who ruled most of India from the 16th to the 19th century, were tolerant and curious about other religions. Mughal artists created artworks illustratrating Hindu themes. They blended Islamic Persian styles with traditional Indian art forms.

During the Raj, many Indians adopted Western dress. In this photograph of the Nehru family, only the mother wears traditional Indian dress. The young boy, Jawaharlal Nehru, grew up to be India's first prime minister.

British influences

By the 1750s, British traders were controlling most of India, and in 1858 India became part of the British Empire. Western-style buildings were built all over the country, and British families brought paintings, ceramics and fabrics from home. Many Indians adopted European dress.

The period when Britain ruled India was known as the **Raj**. Many Indian artists and craft workers produced works for Western tastes.

Textile workers wove cloth with Western designs of flowers, and embroidered tablecloths and handkerchiefs. Metalworkers made silver urns and plates and European-style jewellery. Indian furniture makers were also influenced by Western designs and created delicate chairs and cabinets.

Indian influences

While Indian artists and craft workers were being influenced by Western tastes, Indian decorative arts and architecture were having an impact in Europe. In 1851, the Great Exhibition was held in London. The exhibition was intended as a showcase for the best design in the world and

The Brighton Pavilion was built in southern England in 1782. It was rebuilt from 1815 to 1823 by John Nash, at a time when the British presence in India was becoming more dominant. The building's 'oriental' style was heavily influenced by the Mughal palaces of India.

included a splendid Indian court, filled with examples of Indian crafts. It even featured a model of a ceremonial elephant. In 1875, Liberty and Company opened its Oriental Galleries in London, selling Indian fabrics and ornaments. The galleries were such a success, that in 1890 the company opened a second branch in Paris.

By the 1900s, Indian styles of fabric design and interior decoration had become popular in the fashionable capitals of Europe and in the USA. **Inlaid** metal vases, known as ***bidri***, and inlaid wooden cabinets were especially prized. Women wore embroidered shawls from Kashmir and had decorated cushions and hangings in their homes. A group of artists, now known as the Orientalists, painted exotic scenes of the East, and architects designed buildings with domes and delicate towers based on Mughal palaces.

Changes in painting

During the British Raj, many Indian artists were attracted by European styles of painting, and began to produce landscapes and portraits – subjects that had never been part of the Indian artistic tradition. Painters experimented with watercolours and oil paints and started to show their subjects in a much more **naturalistic** way. By the end of the 19th century, many artists in India were producing paintings that showed Indian people and landscapes in a Western, **Victorian** style.

This strikingly simple portrait of a woman was painted around 1900 by Abanindranath Tagore, one of the founding members of the Bengal School.

The Bengal School

However, not all Indian artists were happy with this new development and during the 1890s, a group of young artists tried to get back in touch with their own traditions. One of the leaders of this group, which became known as the Bengal School, was Abanindranath Tagore. He was influenced by Japanese art, as well as Mughal paintings and Hindu statues, and aimed to create a new kind of 'Oriental art'. Many of the Bengal School painters were involved in the struggle for Indian independence, which was finally achieved in 1947. Their paintings show noble, spiritual figures suffering under the burden of foreign rule.

The early 20th century

In the 1920s, Indian artists began to experiment with contemporary Western styles. In particular, Gaganendranath Tagore was influenced by the **geometric** shapes of **Cubism** - creating magical paintings that played with ideas of light and pattern. Rabindranath Tagore used a **Surrealist** style for his mask-like faces and monsters, which looked like creatures from ancient forests. Amrita Sher-Gil produced striking portraits of poor Indian women that resemble Paul Gauguin's paintings of Taihitian women. Jamini Roy turned to ancient Indian scroll paintings for inspiration in his bold, simplified portraits

Art after Independence

In the same year that India became independent, a Progressive Artists' Group was set up in Mumbai. This group aimed to create modern art with a more worldwide appeal. Over the past 50 years, Indian art has become widely known around the world. Artists work in a range of styles and media, including sculpture and textile art, but their art is usually about India and its people, rather than being purely **abstract**. As India's leading modern artist, M.F. Husain once said, 'How can I go abstract when there are 600 million people around me in India?' Overwhelmed by the abundance of people in India, Husain felt that he could not divorce himself from reality and should focus on real life in his art.

M. F. Husain is a leading contemporary artist who depicts traditional subjects using both Indian and western techniques. Here, his prancing horse is painted in a Cubist style.

◈ Indian style

Indian fabrics, cushions and hangings became very popular in the West during the 1970s, when many young people travelled to India. Since then, Indian art has never really lost its popularity in the West. Indian fabrics, patterns and colours inspire many contemporary fashion and **interior designers**.

Further resources

More books to read

Chatterjee, Manini, and Roy, Anita, *Eyewitness Guides: India* (Dorling Kindersley, 2002)

Dalal, Anita, *Nations of the World – India* (Raintree Steck-Vaughn, 2003)

Shelby, Mamdani, *Traditions from India* (Wayland, 1998)

Websites

http://www.artindia.net/
A site on dance and other performing arts in India

http://www.asia.si.edu/
Indian art collections in the Smithsonian Museum, Washington DC,

http://jigyasa0.tripod.com/
A general site of Indian art, architecture and history with links to Indian Museums and their websites

http://www.roamin-about.com/caves.html
Sculpture and paintings from the caves at Ajanta and Ellora

http://www.taj-mahal.net/
A virtual tour of the Taj Mahal

Places to visit

Europe

British Museum, London

Victoria and Albert Museum, London

Museum van Aziatische Kunst, Amsterdam

USA

Cleveland Museum of Art, Ohio

Harvard University Art Museums, Cambridge, Massachusetts

Metropolitan Museum of Art, New York

Minneapolis Institute of Arts, Minnesota

Museum of Fine Arts, Boston, Massachusetts

Los Angeles County Museum of Art, California

India

Indian Museum, Calcutta

National Museum, New Delhi

Singapore

Asian Civilizations Museum, Singapore

Glossary

abstract art that does not try to be realistic or recognizable

appliqué the technique of stitching cut-out designs on to a larger piece of cloth

Arabs the name given to people who live in the Middle East and North Africa. Most Arabs follow the religion of Islam.

Aryans tribes of people who arrived in India around 1500 BCE. The Aryans were the first Hindus.

Bhagavad Gita a song of the blessed, the most important text in the Hindu religion. It is part of an epic poem, the *Mahabharata*, which was written down around 300 BCE.

bidri metalwork inlaid with coloured enamel

Buddhism a religion based on the teachings of the Buddha and practised mainly in Eastern and Central Asia. Buddhists believe that you should not become too attached to material things and that you live many lives in different bodies.

canopy a small roof or covering made from fabric

capital the top or base of a pillar, that is often decorated with carvings

caste system a system of dividing people into different groups according to the jobs they do. The caste system still survives in parts of India.

commission to pay an artist to produce a work of art

Cubism an early 20th century art movement, in which artists used geometrical shapes

dhoti a cloth that is worn by many Indian men, wrapped around their body

dowry gifts that a bride gives to her husband and takes with her to her new home.

earthenware pots or plates made from baked clay fired at a low temperature

enamel a shiny, glass-like substance that is often inlaid in metal

engrave to cut a design or letters into a surface

epic a long poem or story about heroic adventures or great battles

evaporate to change from a liquid into a vapour

filigree delicate metalwork made from twisted wire

flamboyant bold and showy

fresco painting on walls

fretwork decorative carving including open spaces

geometric featuring regular shapes, such as triangles, squares and circles

Hinduism the main religion of India. Hindus have many gods and believe that they live many lives in different bodies.

Hindustani music a type of classical Indian music practised in the north of the country

incise to cut or carve

inlaid set into the surface of something

inner sanctum the most holy part of a building, such as a temple

interior designer someone who plans the way a building looks inside and chooses flooring, window-coverings and furniture

iris the coloured circle in the centre of an eye

Islam religion based on the teachings of Muhammad. Muslims believe that Allah is God and that Muhammad is his prophet. Their religion is based on prayer, fasting, charity and pilgrimage.

Jainism a religion practised mainly in India. Jains worship many gods and believe that all violence is wrong and that all forms of life are sacred.

jute a plant used for making ropes and sacking

Karnataka music a type of classical Indian music practised in the south of the country (from the region Karnataka)

kiln a very hot oven where pottery is fired

lacquer a hard, glossy coating

Mahabharata a long Hindu poem written down around 300 BCE. It tells the story of two rival families.

maharaja an Indian prince

mausoleum a very large and elaborate tomb

meditate to think about something very deeply

minaret a tall, slender tower of a mosque. Minarets often have a balcony from which Muslims are called to prayer.

mineral a substance found in the earth, that can be obtained by mining

mosque a building used by Muslims for worship

Mughals the Muslim emperors who ruled most of India from 1526 to 1857

Muslim someone who follows the religion of Islam

naturalistic very like the thing it is meant to represent

nirvana a state of perfect peace

ochre a colour made from soil and used for painting or dyeing

pashmina shawl made from fine goat's wool

peninsula a piece of land that sticks out into the sea and is surrounded on three sides by water

pigment a substance that gives colour to something

pilgrimage a religious journey to a holy place

profile the outline of someone's face, seen from the side

promontory a narrow strip of land that sticks out into the sea

raga an Indian word meaning melody or tune

Raj the period when the British ruled India

Ramayana a long Hindu poem written down between the 2nd and 4th centuries BCE. It tells the story of the Hindu god Rama and his wife Sita.

relief carving that stands out from a surface

resist a material such as mud, gum or wax which is painted on to cloth to resist the effect of a dye

rickshaw a two-wheeled passenger vehicle pulled by one or two people

sanctuary an especially holy place in a temple or other religious building

Sanskrit an ancient Indian language

sari a long piece of light material, worn draped around the body. Saris are often worn by Indian women and girls.

shrine a holy building that often includes statues or other holy objects

Sikhism a form of religion practised by some Indians, especially in the Punjab, in northwest India. Sikhs believe in a single god who created the universe. They also believe that all humans are equal.

sitar an Indian stringed musical instrument with a long neck

slip a kind of semi-liquid clay used as paint for decorating pots

soda substance with a high sodium content

stucco a form of plaster that can be moulded or carved into different shapes

stupa a stone or brick dome that contains holy objects. Stupas are built by Buddhists and Jains.

stylized not realistic

Surrealist a 20th century art movement, in which artists created dreamlike images

taal an Indian word meaning rhythm

terracotta an orangey-red clay

tikka an Indian word meaning a circular pendant that is worn on the forehead

trappings saddles, reins and bridles worn by animals

Vedas Hindu holy books, containing ancient hymns

Victorian dating from the period when Queen Victoria reigned, 1837-1901

votive offerings gifts offered to a god to ask for a favour or to give thanks for a blessing

Index

Titles in the World Art & Culture series include:

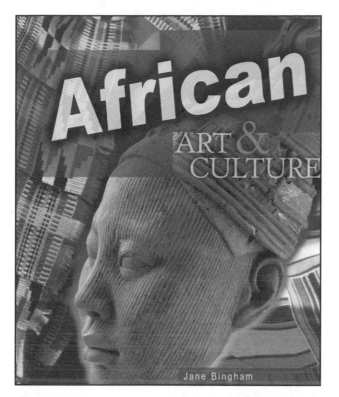

Hardback   1 844 21044 8

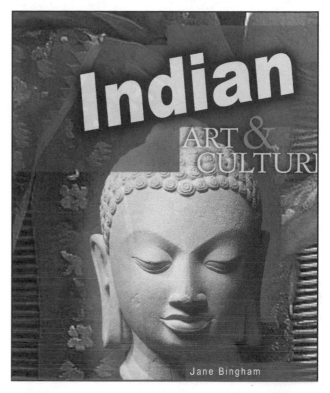

Hardback   1 844 21046 4

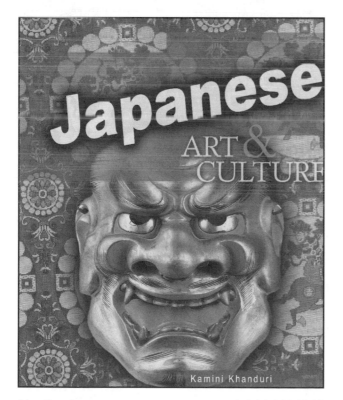

Hardback   1 844 21043 X

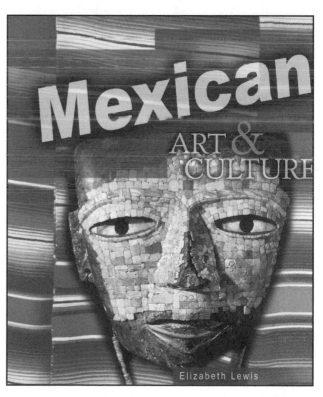

Hardback   1 844 21045 6

Find out about the other titles in this series on our website www.heinemann.co.uk/library